LEGENDS OF LAMPLIT LEWES

A Lewes Ghost Walk and Tales of Other Strange Things

Jane Hasler & Nick Cole

Published by Country Books / Ashridge Press
in association with Spiral Publishing Ltd

Country Books Courtyard Cottage, Little Longstone,
Bakewell, Derbyshire DE45 1NN

Tel: 01629 640670
email: dickrichardson@countrybooks.biz

www.countrybooks.biz

ISBN 978-1-910489-80-2

British Library Cataloguing in Publication Data.
A catalogue record for this book is available from the British Library.

Printed and bound in England by 4edge Limited,
22 Eldon Way Industrial Estate, Hockley, Essex SS5 4AD

Cover picture: Keere Street, Lewes

Dedication

For Nick, a kindred soul. For the good times we had relishing the creating of this walk together and for your friendship. I hope you'd have been pleased with the finished book. You always wished to write and publish books. It is a bit strange to write a dedication to you in a book (much of which you wrote), with ghost stories in it. I think you would appreciate the irony and humour of that.

Socrates said "…death is really a change: a migration of the soul from one place to another."

May your journey have been fair, full of interest, curiosities, adventures and much alliteration!

CONTENTS

CONTENTS

INTRODUCTION

This book is based on work my friend Nick Cole and I did researching, developing and 'performing' this walk a number of times in the1990s, including one event during the Lewes Festival.

Some friends share a unique connection and leave an enduring impression on one's life. Nick was one of those friends for me.

I met Nick in 1994 when working in the Education Department at East Sussex County Council. He was a Substance Misuse Liaison Officer with the Health Authority. We worked together to educate and promote awareness of drug and alcohol issues.

Nick was a great colleague, collaborator and a knowledgeable contributor on our joint work. His warmth, sense of humour, fun and social nature shone through always. His role in drug and alcohol prevention and education with the Health Authority evolved until his sudden passing in 2011.

We both had an interest in history and a curiosity about strange phenomenon and so the idea of a Lewes Ghost walk, 'Legends of Lamplit Lewes' was born. From researching I am aware that there have been other 'ghost walks' in Lewes and, indeed, some paranormal investigations in

Nick Cole and Jane Hasler, Loch Lomond, 2009

different buildings in Lewes. Such things have become of more 'main-stream' interest, perhaps due to recent TV programmes devoted to haunting investigations. This particular compilation is not only ghost stories. It has wider subject matter including saints, fairies, murders, hangings and historical tales and of course, it features a number of accounts of apparitions.

I hope the book will be available to interested people who love Sussex, Lewes and its history to enjoy.

I'd like to add special thanks to Janice, Nick's wife, who steadfastly supported our endeavors, research trips and when we guided folk round the walk.

Nick lived in Lewes, then Eastbourne and had collected strange tales from many sources; books, newspaper articles and, of course, local historical accounts. We met to consider which stories could be in the walk and potential routes. Nick then created the script for the walk, linking the stories up to become the guided walk.

We embarked upon some 'missions' in Lewes to check routes and places. We took the opportunity to check in a few pubs for accounts of ghosts or strange occurrences.

We honed the route and tales after some 'test runs' and feedback from groups of friends.

The stories of some of the hauntings told to us are therefore 'hearsay', and not the result of formal investigations, a **disclaimer** for what you read in the book. Lewes has a rich history and legends, much of which is widely available in multiples sources. Some of these are indicated in the references section. There was also information found on the internet online forums and Nick had his own collection of articles. In preparing to publish this I have changed the narrative which originally addressed the audience present on the walk in theatrical style and also added some extra information/context where it was required. Any historical facts have been checked as far as possible.

Due to the passage of time and not having access to the original articles it has not been possible to give an exact reference for every story included. The reference list included was created by recent desk top research while preparing the book for publication.

We very much enjoyed creating this walk and adventure in history, weaving together strange tales of Lewes. It was done for entertainment purposes for like-minded folk who may be curious about such things. Fundamentally it was for fun and enjoyment. At the time, neither of us knew of any other walks quite like it in Lewes but we had both been on ghost walks in other places.

We were a sight to see on the occasions that we performed the walk. Me, like the black caped 'Scottish Widow' in the TV advert and Nick with his dark mystical cape and characteristic hat, with lanterns escorting the group of assembled folk along the route. My script always included stories with the word "murder" (murrdah), to be said loudly in my strong Scottish accent (which mostly got a laugh!). Nick recounted the stories in his deep, dramatic timbre, relishing the telling of strange and unexpected things. As we only guided the walk a number of times I'm sure he would have been pleased if a book was available for posterity.

The unique illustrations of landmarks and features from some of the stories were created by Kevin Stewart Cantwell BA(Hons). I am grateful for his imagination, help and work to bring some of the streets, stories, buildings and apparitions to life for the reader.

In advance of publication I re-walked the route in late 2019, checking all the places and shops are still where we said they were. There have been some new developments in Lewes since the 1990s. The new Police HQ on the old North Street car park which, in the 1990s, was unbuilt upon. The new Depot Centre has also been built at Pinwell Lane opposite the station.

In early 2020 most of the commercial premises included with tales of hauntings were contacted and sent the story about their premises to be included in the book. While not all replied, quite a few did. It was reassuring that some confirmed the story was as told and at least one responded to indicate there was some recent strange activity continuing!

The physical walk around the streets, lanes and buildings of this amazing county town is an experience in itself. It took me to parts of Lewes and its history that I did not know of, plus a fair few pubs (though not nearly all the pubs in Lewes!). That is for another time where there may be more pub hauntings to be discovered and recounted!

I worked in an office in the attic of Pelham House for a few years when it belonged to East Sussex County Council and I sometimes worked late. However, I never experienced any sign of the apparition included in the story about that particular building.

Preparing for the walk

There is a map of the route and the stops for each story (Story Stops) on the next two pages to help you find your way.

Allow at least two to three hours to walk it, perhaps longer, depending on how many refreshment stops you take. As well as the changes to the town, there is also increased traffic so do follow the route with care especially at any road crossing points.

If walking it at night in the dark, it is advisable to use a torch for any especially dark parts and uneven surfaces. (The book is written with an atmospheric, dark, twilight or evening walk in mind for best effect but the route in daylight is a good experience too .... with clearer views.) It is quite a long walk with some steep bits, narrow paths and passage-ways and a few stairs.

It therefore may not be suitable for anyone with limited mobility or fitness.

Unless it is a commercial premises, e.g. a hotel, public house, tourist site, all other buildings mentioned in the book are not open to the public.

Oh ... and if you are superstitious carry a small sewing pin you are ok to part with!

I hope those who do the walk, whatever time you

choose, enjoy following the tales recounted in this book and beyond… if you dare!

At this point Nick would've probably said, with much gravitas, as he may have done to audiences at the end of our tour, "don't be surprised, if when you do, you discover sinister, strange or spooky things!"

If you have any comments, questions, feedback or know of any further occurrences related to places featured in this book please send them to: **janehslr@me.com**

For any enquiries about the illustrations please contact Kevin Cantwell at: **kevinstewartcantwell@googlemail.com**

ABOUT JANE

I love Sussex, Brighton and Lewes. I lived just outside Brighton and worked in the county for eight years. I started visiting it in 1974/5 when my sister lived in Brighton. My love of the area began then with many regular holidays there until I moved down to live in Brighton in 1994.

Though I ended up back in my native Scotland in 2002, I have visited Sussex very regularly through my life from 1974. It still remains like a second home to me whenever I return which I love to do every so often.

Clock on Lewes High Street

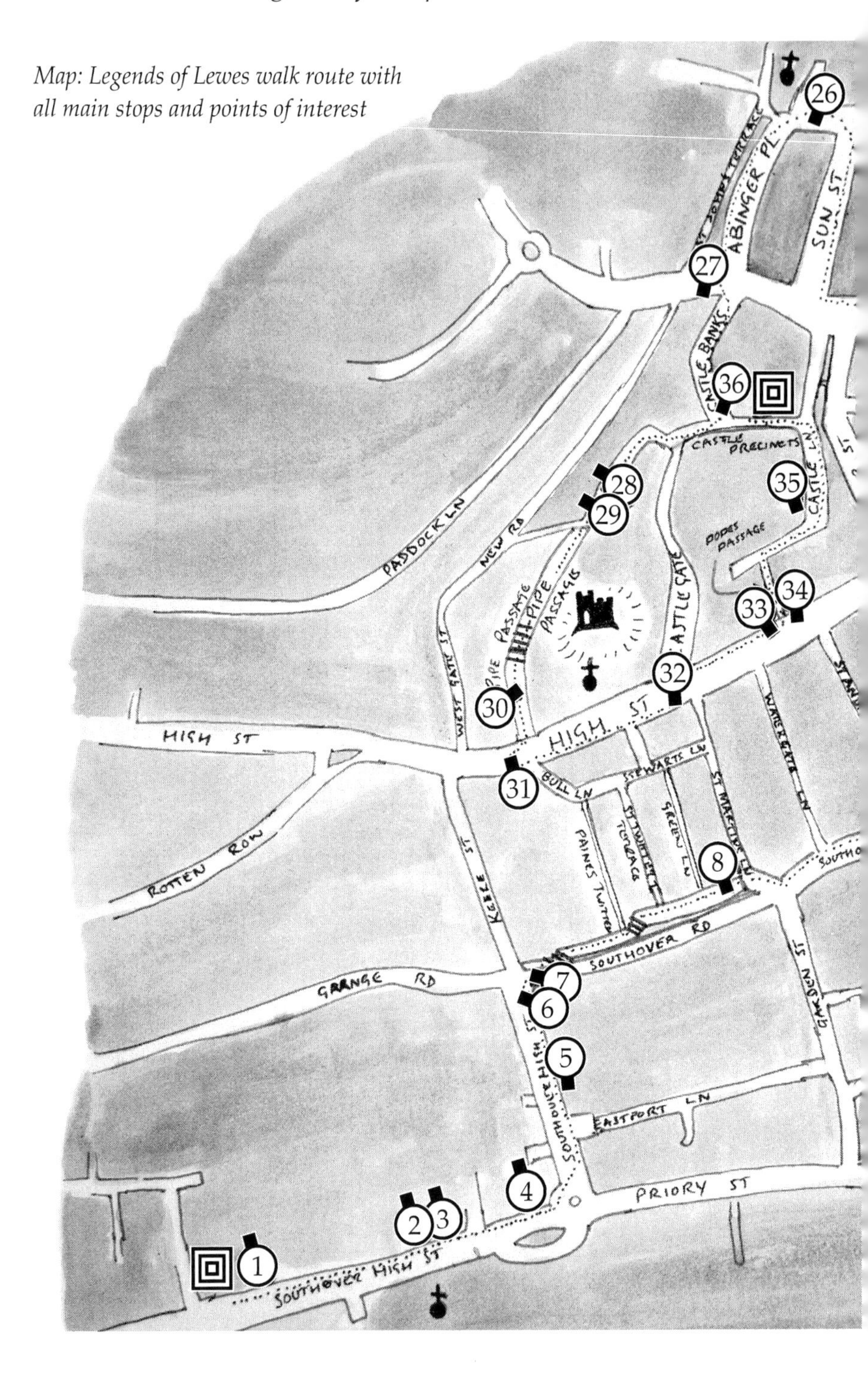

Map: Legends of Lewes walk route with all main stops and points of interest

~ Map ~

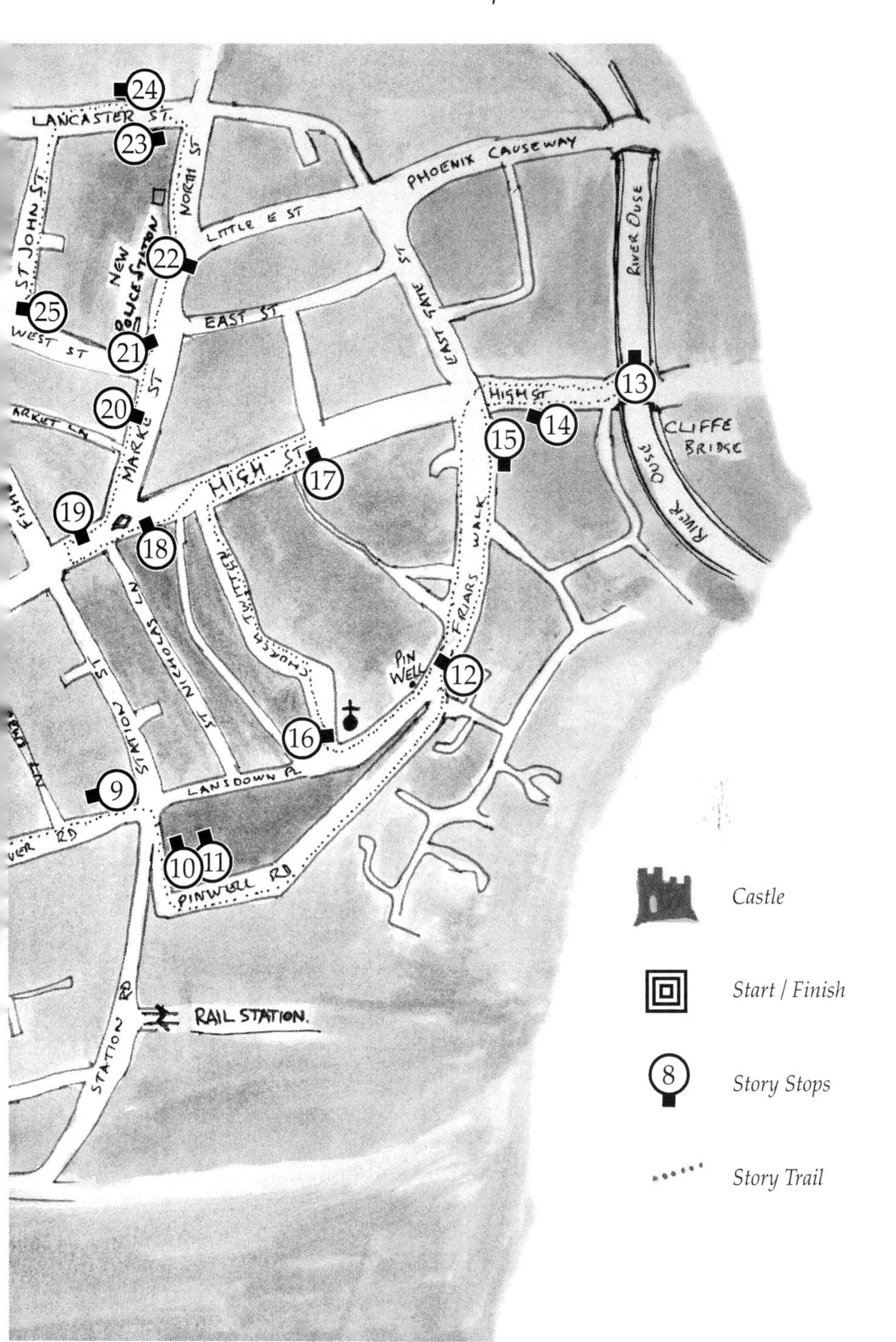

LANCASTER ST.
NORTH ST
PHOENIX CAUSEWAY
RIVER OUSE
LITTLE E ST
ST JOHN ST
NEW POLICE STATION
EAST ST
EAST GATE ST
WEST ST
HIGH ST
CLIFFE BRIDGE
MARKET ST
HIGH ST
FRIARS WALK
RIVER OUSE
CHURCH TWITTEN
ST NICHOLAS LN
STATION ST
PIN WELL
LANSDOWN PL
PINWELL RD
STATION RD
RAIL STATION.
Castle
Start / Finish
Story Stops
Story Trail

1. ANNE OF CLEVES HOUSE HAUNTINGS

Begin at Anne of Cleves House, Southover High Street

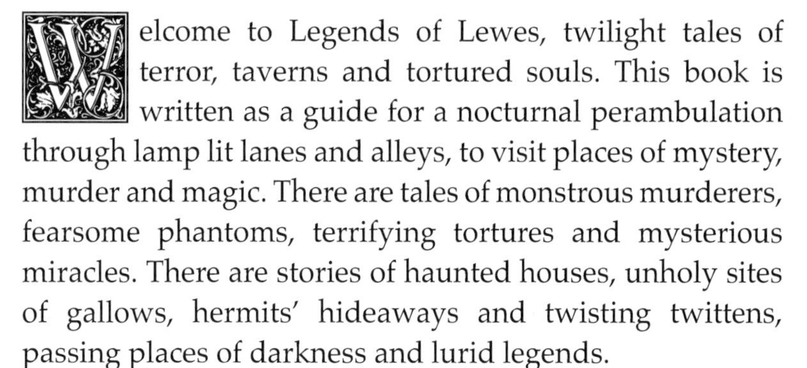

Welcome to Legends of Lewes, twilight tales of terror, taverns and tortured souls. This book is written as a guide for a nocturnal perambulation through lamp lit lanes and alleys, to visit places of mystery, murder and magic. There are tales of monstrous murderers, fearsome phantoms, terrifying tortures and mysterious miracles. There are stories of haunted houses, unholy sites of gallows, hermits' hideaways and twisting twittens, passing places of darkness and lurid legends.

Read on and take a journey of discovery to a haunted theatre, discover where a saint worked a miracle, where martyrs died and one child miraculously returned from the dead.

The journey starts in the Parish of Southover which, in medieval times, was a separate town from Lewes. The building at the start of this walk is known as Anne of Cleves House, although she (the 4th wife of King Henry VIII) never actually lived there. The porch of this ancient house carries the date of 1599 but parts are at least a hundred years older. In earlier days this ancient dwelling had sunk into decay and was shunned as being haunted.

Reports of ghostly apparitions have been encountered

Anne of Cleves House
Southover High Street

in Anne of Cleves House across the years and mentioned in various sources. In the Tapestry Room visitors and staff have experienced inexplicable feelings of intense cold, even on the warmest of days. The wraith of an elderly woman in grey has been seen drifting through the shadows. Custodians of the house have heard footsteps on the stairs in the small hours of the night, the sounds of a man coughing and of a small baby crying coming from the empty rooms. Some visitors reported being terror-struck by seeing a spectral corpse hanging by a rope from a beam on the ceiling. It has in recent times been the subject of a paranormal team's investigation.

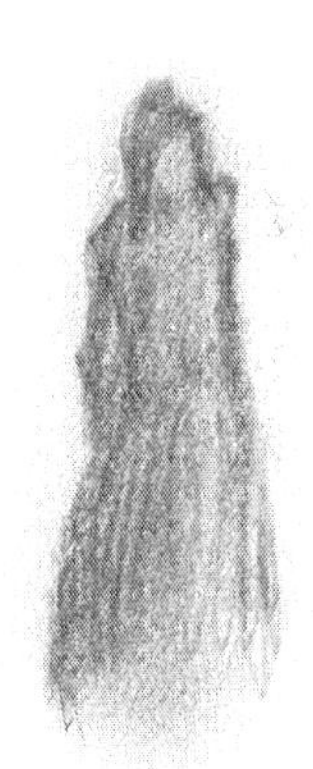

One of the most famous of all the reported hauntings in the house concerns not a person but an item of furniture. Within Anne of Cleves house is a table with a dark history. The table originally stood in Malling Priory, a couple of miles away. It is a weighty table with a heavy wooden frame topped with a solid slab of Horsham marble.

The story goes that after their cowardly murder of Thomas à Becket, the Archbishop at Canterbury in 1170, the guilty knights fled to Malling Priory where they sought sanctuary. Exhausted from their long journey, they flung down their bloodstained clothes and weapons on the great table and sat down to eat. They had only just begun their meals when they were startled by a mighty crash. Every bloodstained item that had been on the table now lay scattered across the floor. They piled the clothes and items back on the table but as soon as they turned away, the same thing happened again. In terror they all fled from the room until daybreak when the knights returned and collected their things and hastily rode off. To this day the table is reputed to be haunted. Perhaps on one December 29th, the anniversary of Becket's murder, it may move once more, still in memory of poor Thomas.

2. SOUTHOVER PARISH CHURCH – WILLIAM AND GUNDRADA

Walk along Southover High Street to the Parish Church of Southover Street

The Parish church of Southover (originally a hospice for Lewes priory). In here were buried the builder of Lewes castle, William de Warenne and his wife the Princess Gundrada, once believed to be the daughter of William the Conqueror (though that has been the subject of subsequent historical debate). Their remains were discovered in the priory ruins in the nineteenth century when the railway was being built. The new rail line cut through the place where the high alter had stood. There were found two lead coffins bearing the names of William and Gundrada. Before the remains were reinterred in 1847 both chests were opened to ascertain if there were any contents – which was found to be the case. New chests were made and the ancient ones preserved and placed in two recesses

Southover Parish Church

in the southern wall of the Norman revival chapel which was erected at that time.

Another oddity was that the great marble lids that should have been on top of both lead coffins were missing. They were discovered having been 'reused' upside down on other tombs in another Sussex village for some 300 years.

3. BATTLE OF LEWES BURIAL PIT

The Lewes to Brighton railway line runs just behind the church and houses through the ruins of the old priory. One day the navvies digging the railway cutting in 1844 were suddenly overcome with the most appalling stench. They had broken into a burial pit in which had been heaped the remains of those slain in the Battle of Lewes in 1264 (a civil war conflict between barons and royalist forces). How many corpses had been piled into the hole originally is impossible to say but no less than thirteen wagon loads of human bones were removed from that terrible pit of death before the building of the railway line could proceed.

4. Kings Head Pub – Strange Occurrences

Continue on Southover High Street and stop at Kings Head Pub

The Kings Head is a pleasant old pub which although advertises as established in the late 1890s, it probably dates back to Tudor times. Strange occurrences were reported to occur in the old building and a mischievous spirit may haunt the place. There is one room which, at times in the past, had been used as a staff changing room and where strange events happened.

Kings Head

Items such as flower petals and burnt matches have been found inexplicably scattered across the floor, although the windows have been closed and the room shut up. From time to time staff and guests in other parts of the building reported hearing the sound of a child crying in the empty room. Peculiar things also happened downstairs in the pub. New landlords were warned that a spirit welcomes newcomers by making its presence known. Objects were thrown from shelves and the kitchen door was seen to swing open or closed by itself. In the kitchen a member of staff was startled to suddenly hear her name called out although she knew she was all alone in the building at the time.

5. SOUTHOVER GRANGE GARDENS – PHOTO PHANTOM

Veer left up Southover High street towards Winterbourne Bridge in the grange gardens. (Look for the stream through the archway in the wall)

Through this archway you can see the Winterbourne stream and the Grange Gardens. One spring day, 50 or so years ago, a lady was out walking in the gardens. The Winterbourne was in full spate and as she had brought her camera with her, she decided to take some pictures of the scene. She was unaware of anything unusual at the time, but when she received the printed photos, she noticed something peculiar in one image. There appeared in the photo to be something she hadn't seen as she took it. The image of man apparently rising out of the rushing waters. He was bent and upon his back he bore some dark burden that seemed to be weighing him down. None of the other pictures of the scene showed the figure. To this day, just who and what she photographed remains a mystery.

Sussex was, of course, part of the routes for pilgrimage by monks particularly in the fourteenth century. One of the most famous destinations then was Canterbury following the murder of Thomas à Becket featured in the first story. Indeed, ghost investigators have reported possible supernatural occurrences that could be related to monks including figures of monks, sounds of chanting and footsteps in a variety of other locations in Sussex. Some of the pilgrims' routes undoubtedly came close to Lewes. In the past there has been at least one monk apparition reported as seen floating across the Grange Gardens here. The Gardens are also not far from the old priory ruins. Since pilgrims journeyed to holy places to be relieved of their sins, could the figure captured in the photo be an ancient monk pilgrim still carrying his burdens on his pilgrim's journey?

6. SOUTHOVER GRANGE – SPECTRAL LIGHTS

Continue up Southover High Street to foot of Keere Street

he fine old building diagonally opposite the bottom of Keere Street is Southover Grange. The ancient house is built with some of the stones from the ruins of nearby Lewes Priory which was demolished by Henry V111 and his lackey minister Thomas Cromwell as part of the huge systematic demolition of monasteries, priories and convents King Henry had ordered.

During the 19th Century the Grange was said to be haunted. For many years the building stood derelict but, especially in winter's twilight, passersby told of seeing the light of a lantern passing silently from window to window in the upper rooms although the old house was barred and locked and no human known to have entered.

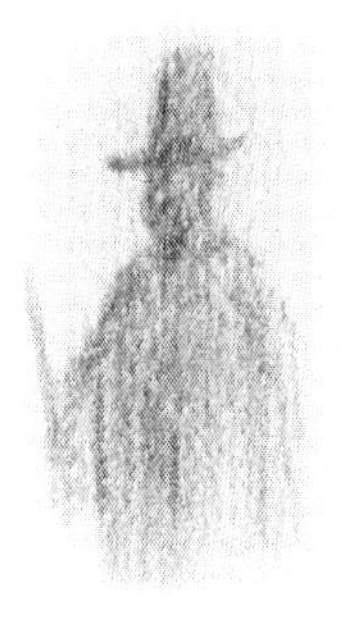

It is also said that a curse is attached to the Grange, that its ownership should never pass from father to the eldest son. Indeed, in the long history of the building, never has the succession passed that way. On every occasion the eldest son has been prevented whether by death, disease, disaster or insanity from coming into his rightful inheritance.

Southover Grange

7. KEERE STREET – THE PRINCE'S WAGER

The steep cobbled hill of Keere Street is perhaps one of the most well-known streets in Lewes and mention must be made of the legendary exploits of George, Prince of Wales who became the Prince Regent in the early 19th century. The Prince often came from Brighton to Lewes to attend races and socialise with friends. He was among other things a great gambler and loved a good wager. One day, it is said, he was bet he could not drive a coach and four horses down Keere St. It is worth remembering that coaches in these days did not have brakes and Keere Street was then a busy street, lined with shops and taverns.

The Prince took up the challenge and much to everyone's terror and amazement hurtled down the hill in his carriage screeching to a halt just outside the Grange. The Prince duly won his bet.

Incidentally (and completely unrelated), the rounded stones with which the street is cobbled are sometimes rather gruesomely known as petrified kidneys. Later on, the route of the walk will take you near the top of this very steep street.

8. THE MABBOTS AND SPRING-HEELED JACK

Across the road from Southover grange (right of Keere Street) walk up steps to foot of St Swithins Terrace and along pathway stopping mid way along near where St Martins Lane adjoins the path

In the nineteenth century this stretch of road was a dim lit tree lined country lane known as 'The Mabbots'.

In the Victorian era there were growing reports of a strange figure or entity, initially in London and then all over the UK, who became known as Spring-heeled Jack.

There are various descriptions of his bizarre tall and

Steps up to St Swithins Terrace/ The Mabbots

cloaked appearance with claw like hands and various other demonic characteristics. He was said to have the ability to leap out high and would terrorise passersby and bound away fast. Some said this was due to powerful springs on his boots.

Lewes, Brighton and other parts of Sussex had reports of Spring-heeled Jack in these times. Whether "Jack" had now become a new way for street robbers to strike is unknown but the name became interchangeable in Victorian times for a street robber who relied on speed and agility to run away after robbing.

The Lewes Spring-heeled Jack allegedly used to hang out here on the Mabbots behind the hedges along this section of the road and leap out at people, particularly courting lovers. He'd bounce about on his spring-loaded boots, and then take off into the dark after well and truly scaring his intended victims.

Who the Lewes Spring-heeled Jack was and why he behaved in this manner is a mystery. In time his exploits became legendary and some parents would tell their children if they were not good girls and boys, Spring-heeled Jack would leap up and in their bedroom windows to grab them away.

9. THE LEWES AVALANCHE

Walk to corner of Station Road and Southover Road

Looking east from this point, in daylight you should see the towering chalk cliffs which give their name to the part of Lewes known as the Cliffe. In the shadow of the actual cliff below is the Snowdrop Inn; but the name has nothing to do with the delicate spring flower. Instead it is a reminder that this was the site of a terrible human calamity.

On Christmas Eve 1836 there had been a steady fall of snow for two whole days. It had been heaped up by the wind into great drifts, some up to 20 feet deep. All the roads in and out of Lewes were impassable. The gale had left a great ridge of snow, ten to fifteen feet thick along the top of the cliff.

Beneath the cliff the inhabitants of Boulder Row and the other dwellings had been warned of the danger posed by the overhanging snow but few, if any, had heeded the warnings. Most of the men folk and younger people had gone out that morning leaving only the very old and young with their mothers at home when the disaster struck. Without warning, at 9.30 in the morning, the mass of snow collapsed and roared down the cliff.

When the clouds of snow which enveloped the houses had cleared, there was nothing left but an enormous mound of pure white snow. Rescuers came at once, some digging with their bare hands into the icy snow. They worked frantically all day until at 4pm, the last of the fifteen victims was dug out. He was lad of just 14 years.

Of the fifteen trapped by the avalanche, eight were killed. Two of the survivors were infants of six weeks old, one still in its dead mother's lap. It remains to this day the greatest avalanche disaster in British history. The Snowdrop Inn, originally built in 1840, marks the site of the tragedy.

Intersection between Pinwell Road/Lane and Station Street

10. RAILWAY TALES I: 1851 RAILWAY DISASTER

Turn right onto Station Road then immediately cross road and take sharp, narrow road sloping down to left into Pinwell Road, stop opposite station. (Take care as traffic can turn down this road)

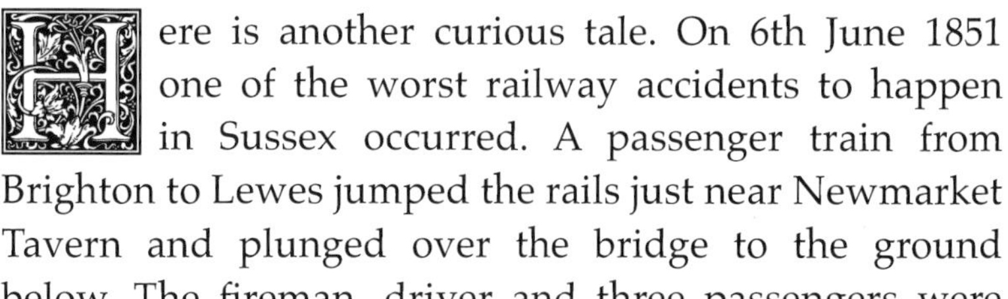

Here is another curious tale. On 6th June 1851 one of the worst railway accidents to happen in Sussex occurred. A passenger train from Brighton to Lewes jumped the rails just near Newmarket Tavern and plunged over the bridge to the ground below. The fireman, driver and three passengers were tragically killed. It soon became clear that this disaster had been no accident. A heavy wooden sleeper had been placed across the track causing the train to be derailed. A young shepherd lad came under suspicion and he was arrested and questioned but there was no evidence to bring charges and he was released. That might have been the end of the matter, but there was a bizarre sequel to this disaster. Exactly one year later on the anniversary of the accident, at almost exactly the same place, the same youth was struck by lightning and killed. A co-incidence perhaps? Or divine justice?

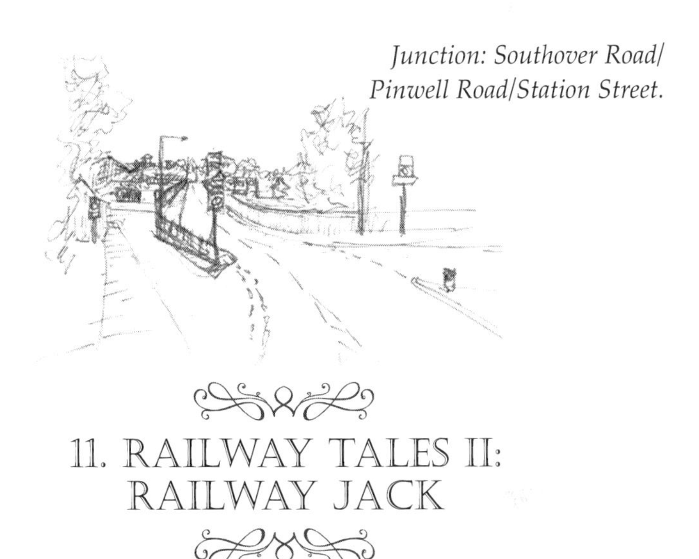

Junction: Southover Road/ Pinwell Road/Station Street.

11. RAILWAY TALES II: RAILWAY JACK

Another railway related story is the curious and heart-warming tale (or should it be tail?) of Railway Jack, the three-legged fox terrier who lived here in the 1880s, adopted by Mr Moore the station master. Jack, it turned out, was an avid train traveller and took trains to local stations, always finding his way back to Lewes without help from the railway staff. His solo journeys covered most of the stations served by the London, Brighton and South Coast Railway, frequently changing trains.

But Jack was also no ordinary travelling dog as he appeared to also have second sight. When his friend Inspector Bryant died, Jack found his way without guidance to Eastbourne where he followed the funeral procession. He also turned up uninvited to the wedding of another friend to attend the celebrations. Jack was a famous dog indeed and was presented to the Prince and Princess of Wales in 1883.

12. THE PIN WELL AND FAIRY FOLK

Continue along Pinwell Road passing the 'Depot' centre to the end of the lane stopping at the junction with Friars Walk

he lane you have walked down is called Pinwell Road or Lane. At the end of it across the Street you will see an ornate Victorian drinking fountain built into the wall. This fountain is a reminder that this used to be a place of sorcery and power. It was the site of a magic spring called the Pin Well which gushed forth at this place in olden days.

The well was said to be guarded by the mysterious beings known to Sussex folk as the Pharisees. The guardians of the well would ward off evil spirits in exchange for the gift of a pin dropped into the flowing water.

Looking down Pinwell Lane

The Pharisees are fairy beings of old Sussex but they are not the delicate fairies with gossamer wings of popular imagination. One old man described a Pharisee as a 'little creature, rather bigger than a squirrel, and not quite as big as fox'. But whether human or semi human in appearance, they were held in awe and reverence by the people of Sussex in olden times.

Before moving on, if you are superstitious, it would be wise to drop a token of a pin into the well and say:

'Oh, Pharisees of the Pin Well,
we humbly offer you your
chosen token to keep us safe
this day/night in Sussex.'

13. CLIFFE BRIDGE MIRACLE

Turn right, continue along Friars Walk. At the pedestrian shopping area, turn right and walk to Cliffe Bridge

ussex has been the home of many Saints but the greatest of all and the one most associated with Lewes and Sussex is St Richard de la Wyche who was born in 1197. Many tales are told of the good Saint Richard and one of them recalls a miracle which happened at Cliffe Bridge. One day as Saint Richard was crossing the bridge he passed a group of men who were fishing in the river. They greeted him as he passed and he asked them what they had caught. They replied that they had been there since daybreak and they had caught nothing. They asked the Bishop to stop a while with them as perhaps he would bring better fortune. Saint Richard smiled at this and raising his hand, blessed both the men and the water saying, "now cast your nets in the name of The Lord." They did so and instantly drew up four big and beautiful mullet which Saint Richard told them to take as offerings to the Grey Friars in the Priory nearby. Thereafter for the reminder of the day the fishermen's nets were filled again and again until enough had been caught for the needs of everyone.

Cliffe Bridge

14. UNLIKELY PLACE FOR A HAUNTING

Walk back to the pedestrian precinct and stop opposite the M&Co and Clarkes of Sussex shops on left hand side when facing towards School Hill

This very ordinary looking row of modern shops seems an unlikely spot for a haunting but in years gone by strange things were reported to happen within their walls.

Staff working at what is now Clarkes of Sussex reported hearing strange sounds from the upstairs stockroom. Footsteps were heard crossing the ceiling above and doors banged shut, even though it was known there was no-one else in the building. On one occasion, a handbag was seen to slide of its own accord across a table and tumble to the floor.

At M&CO equally strange things were reported to happen. Staff reported hearing footsteps from the room overhead, this time more like the sound of a child's feet running. On other occasions, staff have found themselves shut in the stock room when the door slammed shut for no apparent reason whilst they were inside. The atmosphere in the room was described as unnerving. A locksmith who was called in to check the troublesome door complained he was perturbed as all the time he was working on the door he felt he was silently being watched.

At one time the old Tabernacle Chapel stood here and before that a Quaker burial ground. In the middle ages the land formed part of the Priory of the Grey Friars, (after which Friars Walk was named). Could there be a ghost of a medieval Friar responsible for these strange occurrences or maybe a Quaker child?

While preparing to publish this book, the Manager of Sussex Books reported back: 'Myself and staff were quite surprised, as odd noises have been coming from the first floor, which is now our Toy department, and several jokes have been made regarding ghosts, unaware that there was any documentation regarding this.' And so the mystery continues.

One other story to tell about this location. During a great flood of 1960, when the Winterbourne burst its banks, strange thudding sounds were heard coming from the crypt beneath the old chapel building. Eventually a few brave souls decided to investigate, breaking down the heavy wooden door, they forced their way into the vault.

There they found the cause of the sounds. They witnessed the spectacle of dozens of coffins floating about and bumping into each other in the dark waters of the flooded crypt.

15. ANOTHER MIRACLE

Turn left into Friars Walk by the Magistrate Court. Stop where there is a historical sign for the old Friary on the building wall

There is a tale of another miracle which took place near here. It was at the Cliffe, near the Friary which stood upon this site, that a young girl was brought from the grave by the miraculous power of prayer. In the hot summer of 1498, the plague was once again rife and many were dying in Lewes. A poor lass name Joan Reynolds had fallen ill and died. Joan's lifeless body was sewn up within its shroud and ready for burial when her grief-stricken parents made one desperate prayer to the spirits of the saints. No sooner had they finished their prayers when they noticed Joan's body move. Tearing off the shroud they found her restored to life and health.

16. ALL SAINTS HAUNTING

Walk along Friars Walk which becomes Lansdown Place back to All Saints Centre

he old church here is All Saints Centre. It has not been used as a church for many years but has been an arts centre and venue for music. It was here one hot August night in 1974 that two young people had a terrifying experience. The young man, Gary, had been playing in a band that evening. He and his girlfriend Theresa were packing away the equipment after the gig. As they were all alone, they stopped for a kiss – a kiss which turned to terror. Suddenly they heard eerie footsteps and felt an intense and clammy coldness, despite the heat of the night. They both felt as if something or someone was holding them down. Gary grabbed the drum stand and formed it into a makeshift crucifix and they were able to somehow break free and run outside. The lights were still on in the building and he ventured back in. This time he was hurled from his feet and back out through the door by some unseen force. The two of them jumped into Gary's van and drove away as fast as they could. But there was yet one more bizarre turn, Teresa felt a burning sensation and found that her wristwatch had become very hot and was burning her arm. In great distress they drove to the police station and were so evidently upset that the police returned

Lansdowne Place/All Saints

to search the building. But of course, nothing was found. There has been no record of any haunting before or since (as far as can be known) so why two young people were afflicted on that evening all those years ago will no doubt remain a mystery.

Church Twitten

17. ICE CREAM LIL & THE TALE OF ROBERT BRINKHIRST (PART 1)

Turn up Church Twitten to the right. Go to the very top. Turn right down School Hill to Temple House (look for the Temple House sign on the building, just one up from Sea Salt shop)

This is Temple House, a modern building which housed the office of a local newspaper. Hardly a likely place for a haunting, but in past years, journalists working there late into the evening experienced strange and intense feelings of cold especially in one particular office. Although feelings of cold are often associated with ghosts, in this case there is thought to be a special reason why they are shivering. The building is believed to be haunted by the spirit of Ice Cream Lil. Before the present building, this was the site of the old Cinema De Luxe, affectionately known as the 'fleapit'. Lil was the ice cream lady for many years. Where her kiosk once stood is the advertising office and it is in there and the room immediately below that the icy temperatures were experienced. For some reason Ice Cream Lil may well be still trying to sell her wares from the next world.

The name of Temple House is a reminder that in middle ages, the mysterious Knights Templar had a church in what is now Albion Street. Many bizarre legends are associated with the Templars; that they possessed the Holy Grail, or the Ark of the Covenant, that they worshipped a severed head called Baphomet.

The circular church of Saint Sepulchure in Lewes was lost after the Templars were disbanded by the Pope at the start of the fourteenth century. The memory of the crusaders lingers on in the name of the Turks Head Inn which later stood on this site but is also no longer here.

The Turks Head, in the seventeenth century, doubled as the local courthouse. It was here that the tragic tale of Robert Brinkhurst came to a climax when he took poison in a desperate attempt to cheat the hangman and to die by his own hand. It is a sad tale of jealousy, murder and forbidden love that had begun some years earlier.

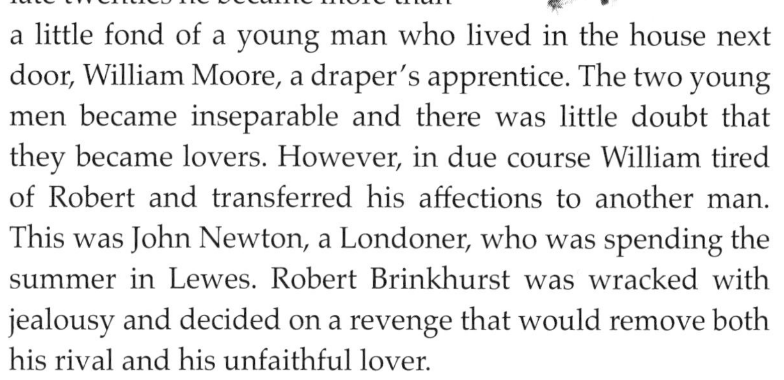

Robert was a moderately well off merchant who lived not far from here on the High Street. He was unmarried but in his late twenties he became more than a little fond of a young man who lived in the house next door, William Moore, a draper's apprentice. The two young men became inseparable and there was little doubt that they became lovers. However, in due course William tired of Robert and transferred his affections to another man. This was John Newton, a Londoner, who was spending the summer in Lewes. Robert Brinkhurst was wracked with jealousy and decided on a revenge that would remove both his rival and his unfaithful lover.

Robert devised a plot in which arsenic would be sent to William, apparently from John Newton. It would be disguised as a medicine for William's halitosis, from which he suffered badly.

At first the plot seemed to work. William took the poison, sickened and took to his deathbed as his supposed friend Robert Brinkhurst looked on. As William died a slow and agonizing death, it became evident he had been murdered. Suspicion first fell on John Newton, as Robert had intended, but soon he became the chief suspect. He was arrested and brought here to the Turks Head Inn to be tried for the murder of William Moore. But Brinkhurst was not willing to die on the gallows and tricked the court into providing him with a sample of the arsenic which he grabbed and swallowed. This is not quite the end of the story. We will come back to the end of this sad tale in due course.

18. LEWES MARTYRS

Walk up School Hill to War Memorial

It was at this place that perhaps one of the darkest episodes in the long history of the town took place. The story of the Lewes Martyrs is well known; here, where today stands the war memorial, in the years of 1556 and 1557, seventeen men and women were burned alive at the stake for professing the Protestant faith. We can only imagine the horror of the scene as they were shackled to posts stacked round with wood and straw and the fires lit.

The large brick building to the left on the opposite side of the road is the old Town Hall which stands on the site of the old Star Inn. Those poor souls awaiting execution were kept imprisoned in the cellars of the Inn. The Inn has a long gone but below the ground, however, the vaults remain in which the Lewes Martyrs awaited their doom. Through a glass insert on the pavement just outside the town hall, you can see the stairs

War Memorial, Lewes High Street

that each of the Martyrs would have mounted as they went to their deaths and a plaque above it.

Also according to legend, the cellars under the Star formed part of a network that ran to the White Hart and to the Crown Hotel / Inn, a building nearby (now closed as an Inn). There have been reports of paranormal activity in the past with staff avoiding going down to the cellars alone at night if they could, such was the uneasy atmosphere of that network of the underground areas said to be.

19. HA BAKER - SHOP HAUNTING

Cross over to the Town Hall side of the road past the Martyrs Steps and look over to HA Baker the chemist

very ordinary chemist shop may seem an unlikely place for a ghost but it appears this may be haunted. The date of the building is 1613 and shows that it is an old building.

Staff and customers have reported on occasions a ghostly figure of a young woman. She is usually in the same area of the shop. Several people have drawn the figure which is that of a young woman with her hair coiled into a bun, clad in a long Victorian style dress.

Market Street

20. PRINTING PRESSES STILL ROLLING?

Turn left down Market street. Stop opposite building called Farncombe House

Earlier you read the tale of the haunted newspaper offices. There is a building here on the right hand side of the street called Farncombe House. It was formerly the newspaper offices and the print works of the Sussex Express. This too allegedly had a ghost. People working here back in the 1970s regularly heard ghostly feet on the stairs, experienced doors opening and closing by themselves and even heard the toilet flushing when it was unoccupied. Some people believed this spirit to be the one time Head Printer who cannot rest and returns to his place of work.

21. A YOUNG GHOST'S SAD STORY

Continue on Market St and cross over West Street, stop near the Chalk Gallery and Clock Makers shops

his building (4-5 North St) is now the Chalk Gallery and W Bruce's Clock Makers but magician and entertainer, Tony Richards, better known as `Tony Lusion', bought it in 1995. Not long after his family moved in strange things were reported to happen. Bizarre sounds were heard in the building at night as though someone was walking around downstairs. Several times family members heard their names being called out although they were alone in the building. There were also sounds of breaking glass. The radio would suddenly turn on and off when no-one was near it. Inexplicable shadows were seen to be passing across the floor, on at least one occasion resembling a small boy.

The haunting is believed to possibly be the spirit of a young lad who was killed in World War II. His name was Stanley Johnson and he was nine years old. During a huge air raid on January 20th 1943 a bomb detonated across the road and the child was caught in the full blast which hurled him across the street and through the window into the shop. The haunting seems only to have begun when the Richards moved into the house. Was poor Stanley trying to reach out the children who reminded him of his lost childhood?

As a sad footnote, Tony Lusion died in 1996 and his family moved on.

22. THE GUESTLING MURDERESS

Continue straight onto North Street near to site of old North Street car park (now new Police Building)

This car park and new Police building occupies the site of the original Lewes prison. This spot, just opposite Little East Street was also the site of the Gallows in the nineteenth century. There are too many tales to tell of this place but just one will suffice; the tale of Mary Ann Geering, a cold murderess and yet also a sad figure of pity, who breathed her last on August 21th 1849.

Mary Ann was born in 1800 near Battle. At the age of 18 she was sent out to service and soon was walking out with a handsome young farmhand named Richard Geering. Mary Ann soon found that she was pregnant and so entered a marriage that in later years began to deteriorate. They raised eight children and lived in Guestling in East Sussex but the marriage was continually stormy. They were constantly on the brink of poverty but one act of prudence was their regular payments to the Friendly Society which provided benefit payments in case of sickness or death. Also, in 1846 Richard was left a sum of £20 which he deposited in Hastings savings bank which he and Mary Ann often quarreled about.

One day in September 1848, just after another of their furious rows, Richard Geering was suddenly taken ill and died two days later. The Doctor signed the certificate that he had died of a disease of the heart and Mary Ann collected £5 1s 4d in funeral expenses from the Friendly Society.

Soon one of their sons fell ill with similar symptoms. His mother tended him but he lapsed into a coma and died. Six weeks after his death, another son became ill with a similar ailment and died despite his mother's attentions. Each time there was a death Mary Ann received the insurance money from the Friendly Society although each funeral was conducted with as little expense as possible.

When three weeks later a third son was struck down with the same illness it appeared that the Geering family was cursed. Or was something more sinister going on? The Doctor believed so and against his mother's wishes removed the youth from Mary Ann's care. Almost at once the young man's condition improved and he was soon restored to health. The speediness of his recovery prompted great suspicion that she had fed poison to her husband and sons. Their bodies were exhumed and found to contain traces of arsenic. The savings money had also been drawn out after Richard's death. Mary Ann Geering was tried at Lewes Asssizes on 7th August 1849, found guilty of three charges of willful murder and one attempted murder and was sentenced to be hanged.

Imagine, if you will, the morning of August, the 28th 1849 a huge crowd of several thousand gathering in Lewes as people flocked to see the 'Guestling Murderess' die. The hour of noon approached on a hot August day. The

crowd becomes restless. Suddenly the execution party appears: Mary Ann bareheaded and dressed all in black supported by two jailers. She slowly mounts the steps to the gallows. The crowd falls silent leaving only the sound of the priest's voice praying for her soul.

The Executioner then steps forward to complete his task; the hood drawn over Mary Ann's head, the rope fixed around her neck and passed over the crossbeam. Her hands were not tied and she clasps them together as if in prayer. For a moment time seems to stand still, then with awful suddenness the silence broken by the bolt being drawn back and Mary Ann plunging into the dark oblivion of death.

Before her death Mary Ann made full confession of her crimes. It seems incredible that she would have killed her husband and sons for a few pounds of insurance but such was the case. Who can tell if the 'Guestling Murderess' or Murdering Mother as she became known would have taken more of her children's lives?

23. OLD PRISON AND GALLOWS SITE

Continue along North Street turning left into Lancaster Street and go up a little way until the Little Theatre is on right hand side

Corner of Lancaster and North Street

pposite the Little Theatre stood the main entrance to the prison and it was through here that so many men and women would pass, many on their final journey. Look carefully to the right and you can clearly see the remains of the huge old prison walls. It is not difficult to imagine the scene with the gallows beyond rising above the wall and the thronging crowds below.

Across on the other side of the street, in what is now the car park of the Little Theatre, stood the Crimean Tavern directly opposite the great north entrance gate. The pub was named after the Russian prisoners of war who were held captive in the prison, many of whom now lie buried in the graveyard of the church of St John sub Castro.

24. LITTLE THEATRE – AN ECCLESIASTICAL SPIRIT

Many theatres are said to be haunted and the Little Theatre is no exception. Over the years there have been accounts of footsteps in the deserted gallery and experiences of sudden feelings of icy cold. The Little Theatre was converted from a disused chapel in 1939 and perhaps that is why the most bizarre incident happened when there is a play on a religious theme being performed. The story goes that some 50 years ago a play based on the life of Luther (a German theologian and priest) was being staged which involved the cast appearing as monks dressed in black habits. After each performance, the wardrobe mistress laid out the costumes carefully labelled for each actor. Each night the habits were moved around with the result that the shorter cast members were tripping over their overly long garb and the taller ones had habits just around knee length. Some costumes disappeared altogether and only reappeared months later in the stalls.

25. POLICE ENQUIRIES CONTINUING

Walk up St John Street on the left to the Old Police station near the top of the street

re ghosts of police officers past haunting the old Lewes Police station? Rumours have abounded for 60 or more years of ghostly presences.

In 1968 a group of Police officers allegedly held a séance in the station. They linked hands and called out the names of police commemorated as dying in World War 1. They were more than startled when they heard a faint voice replying: "Yes I can hear you, my name is Leonard Budd." Leonard was one of the officers who was recorded as having lost his life in the Great War. Alarmed the group rapidly ended that séance.

When still in use as the Police Office, various officers reported unexplained and weird experiences, focused on the first floor of the building which was usually unoccupied at night at that time. Closed doors were observed to open inexplicably, the face of a man was seen looking from an upper window and strange footsteps have been heard from the empty first or second floors. A spectre was also seen once downstairs; he was described as gaunt, slim, in his early 50s and dressed in a Chief Inspector's uniform. One woman officer spoke to him as he walked past but he ignored her and then vanished before her eyes.

Old Police Station

The living boys and girls in blue apparently took the matter seriously enough back then to have sought spiritual guidance from the Police chaplain. Are Police enquiries continuing?

26. HERMIT'S HIDING PLACE

Turn right, then right again to walk down Sun Street towards St John Church (left at the bottom of the street)

The Church of St John Sub Castro, (meaning St John under the castle) is the site of the next story. The building you see is a Victorian structure but it stands on the site of a much older church. It was here that it is said that a Danish Prince, named Magnus lived and died as an anchorite. In the walls of the church you

Church of
St John Sub Castro

can still see the archway that led to Magnus's cell. After he had entered the doorway would have been blocked up save for a tiny window through which he could receive food and drink and most importantly, receive the sacrament. Over the doorway you will clearly see the inscription reads:

"Here is immured a soldier of the Royal family of Denmark. Relinquishing his greatness, he assumes the deportment of a lamb, and exchanges a life of ambition for that of a humble anchorite."

But who was Prince Magnus and why should a Royal Prince of Denmark end his days as a hermit in a church in Lewes? No-one knows but there are legends. Some say he was the son of King Harold, (the last crowned Anglo-Saxon King of England in 1066). Magnus may have hidden himself here in the guise of anchorite if his father had been slain in the Battle of Hastings, to avoid the undoubtedly murderous intentions of the Norman conquerors. But it has also been whispered over the centuries that King Harold did not die on the battlefield but fled to safety and ended his life as a hermit. Could it be that it was here at this very place that the last Saxon King of England or his son, Magnus, hid from the world until a lonely death?

27. HANGMAN'S ACRE AND SAINT RICHARD'S JUSTICE

Walk back along Abinger Place and stop near the Elephant and Castle pub opposite Castle Banks

Near where the Elephant and Castle pub stands was the site of the very original ancient gallows. Here was also the site of the parish stocks where wrong doers were punished and publicly humiliated. The field opposite was known as Hangman's Acre and its rental provided income for the hangman to carry out his grisly duties. When the present road was being constructed in the middle of the 19th Century another burial pit full of human skeletons were unearthed here. These may have been the remains of the victims of the Battle of Lewes or the Black death or the Hangman.

Another tale of St Richard de la Wyche is said to have happened at the site of the gallows. Saint Richard was known as a man of peace but he was also a man of justice and when wrong had been done, he was a fearsome opponent. One day a thief had been at work in town, robbing a number of wealthy citizens. They chased him across the town in order to catch him. The terrified thief fled as fast as he could into a church and flung himself down before the alter claiming sanctuary. In those days the right of church sanctuary was absolute. However, the pursuing mob dashed straight into the church, dragged the thief from the sacred place and took him to the gallows and hanged him without further ado. His body they buried there in unconsecrated ground.

When Saint Richard heard of this he was filled with fury, for what they had done was a violation of the laws of God. Saint Richard gathered all the guilty before him and they were forced to return to the spot where they had buried the thief two weeks earlier and to exhume the corpse.

After a fortnight in the ground it was decaying, stinking and foul but they had to carry it, putrid as it was, through the town to the church whose sanctuary had been violated. There, with their bare hands, they had to rebury the corpse in sacred ground. Then, just to underline his point, St Richard made them parade through the streets of the town bare foot with nooses round their necks.

Castle Banks

28. CASTLE PRECINCTS – VICTORIAN LADY

Cross the road up Castle Banks. At top of the hill veer right where there is good view point at Castle Precincts looking over parts of Lewes. When clear, the current prison can be seen

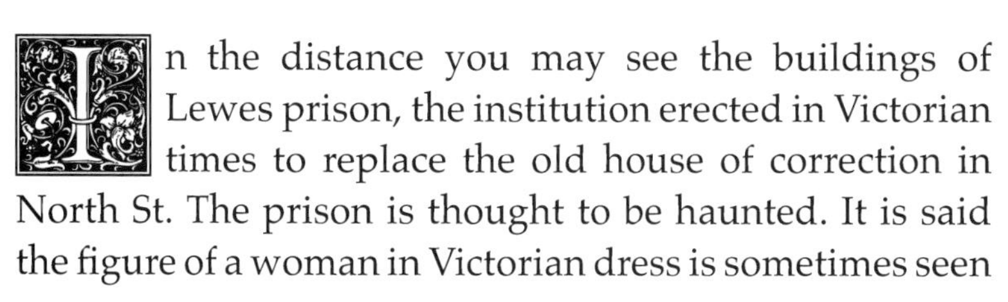

In the distance you may see the buildings of Lewes prison, the institution erected in Victorian times to replace the old house of correction in North St. The prison is thought to be haunted. It is said the figure of a woman in Victorian dress is sometimes seen drifting through the corridors. It is thought she may be the ghost of a lady visitor who was so shocked by the conditions in which the inmates were incarcerated that she collapsed with a brain fever and died on the spot. But the prison was also once the place for burials for those who had committed suicide as we shall hear further on in these tales.

29. CASTLE PRECINCTS – OLD TOWN WALLS

Continue ahead via the narrow path. The path drops down onto an adjacent road where steps go up to the left will take you back up and into Pipe Passage

The path from Castle Banks / Precincts to Pipe Passage formed part of the old town walls of Lewes. Where you may now tread in centuries past guards and watchmen patrolled alert for enemies. Some say that on a still night the spirits of those guards can still be heard to pass along the walls on their endless patrol.

30. PIPE PASSAGE – TOBACCO KILN

Continue down Pipe Passage towards High Street

This twitten is known as Pipe Passage because at one time a kiln on the site produced clay pipes for the Lewes folk to smoke their baccy. You will see the historical information about the pipe kiln further along the passage. When the passage comes out onto the High Street, you can see a unique old book shop building across the road which sits at the corner of the very steep and narrow Keere Street. You passed the lower end of that street and read the story for the Prince Regent and Coach and Fours bet. It is worth a look from the top to see just how steep it is.

Looking up Pipe Passage from High street

31. THE TALE OF ROBERT BRINKHURST (PART 2)

Cross over to entrance to Stewards Inn Lane at High Street near Brewers Arms Pub

ow to return to the tale of Robert Brinkhurst. The ancient coaching inn known as the White Horse used to stand close by here in the High Street, in the shadow of the Castle. It was here, at six o'clock on the evening of Saturday Dec 6th 1679 that Robert Brinkhurst died in terrible agony, slain by his own hand. It was almost, but not quite, the final act in this tragedy.

Robert, as you will recall, had taken arsenic to cheat the hangman, having already poisoned his former lover William Moore out of jealousy for taking up with someone else. As the poison worked on him and he sickened, he was removed from the Turks Head and dragged up the High Street here to the White Horse Inn where he finally died.

It was not quite the end of the tale; Robert's family brought a coffin and asked to have him buried in the graveyard at Saint Michaels Church and when that was refused by the authorities, they asked at least to be able to bury him in a plot of their own land.

But there was a more awful fate reserved for the remains Robert Brinkhurst who had perpetrated the double sins of suicide and murder. On Monday morning

Old Book Shop, High Street

his half naked corpse was flung onto a dung cart and dragged around the town to the crossroads near where the modern prison stands. There his body would have been thrown into a shallow pit and a wooden stake driven through his bowels before being heaped over with earth and dung. Upon the protruding stump of the stake was fixed a brass plate as a reminder of the terrible deeds committed by Robert Brinkhurst.

32. CASTLE GATE – A MEDIEVAL GHOST STORY

Cross back to other side of road, walk further down High Street to Castle Gate which is to the left

ere is the massive gateway of Lewes Castle but seven hundred years ago according to a legend, it was not enough to protect a wicked man from his fate. It was near midnight on a sultry August night in the year 1307. A storm had been brewing all day. High in his chamber in the castle Lord Eustace de Warenne could not sleep. Down below at the gate the guards kept watch. The drawbridge had been raised for the night and the mighty gates bolted shut.

Suddenly there was the sound of hooves and a troop of horsemen, all clad in black, rode up to the gate demanding to see the Earl. The guards refused, whereupon an unseen hand severed the chains that held the bridge whilst another drew back

Castle Gate

the mighty bolts of the gates. The horsemen rode into the castle.

In his chamber Earl Eustace suddenly looked up and saw a tall helmeted figure standing before him. Eustace demanded to know who stood before him. The knight remained silent but slowly removed his helmut. As he did so Eustace fell back in terror, for the face was that of his elder brother who was the Earl before him. He had died on his wedding day two years before.

The ghostly knight summoned Eustace to attend a banquet in the Great Hall. The hall was all lit up with torches. On either side were ranks of silent, black armored men but when Eustace looked, he saw their faces were eyeless skulls. Before him stood the ghosts of his brother and his brother's bride. In terror Eustace ran and leapt upon one of the black horses which instantly galloped away. But as it did so there was a great crash. The storm broke and a bolt of lightning struck the castle tower. The great walls collapsed and crushed Eustace to death as he rode away. The castle fell into disrepair for many years.

So was the truth that Eustace had murdered his brother, the rightful earl, and his bride upon their wedding knight so as to inherit the earldom and lands? If this story sounds fantastic, many years later when the castle was being rebuilt, the skeletons of a man mounted on a horse were uncovered on the spot where Eustace was said to have died.

33. THE WHITE HART – SOME APPARITIONS

Continue along High Street to opposite White Hart / St Andrews Lane

The White Hart is one of Lewes's oldest inns and it would be surprising if such an ancient inn did not have one or two ghosts within its walls. Indeed, it is reputed to have some. Guests have sometimes been surprised late at night to see an elderly porter apparently at his duties but it is no living person they have seen. It is believed to be the spirit of a man who many years ago was a night porter at the hotel and who seems, for some reason, unable to leave his duties.

Other accounts have been of a circle of ghostly men in conversation – appearing to suddenly look up if observed and then disappear.

Another figure has also startled a few guests, described only as a lady in grey, she silently drifts along the passageways of the second floor.

34. PELHAM HOUSE – GREY LADY

The narrow street to the right of the White Hart is Saint Andrews Lane. On the right hand side further down the hill stands Pelham House

The house, once used as the Council chambers and offices for East Sussex County Council in the 1990s, is now a hotel but its foundations go back five hundred years or so. It was a place with narrow passage ways and back stairs. Pelham House was said by some who worked there in the 1990s to have its own grey lady, a shadowy figure who startled people working late and alone in the building. Those who have seen her

Pelham House (from garden)

describe her as Victorian in appearance but she could be from older times. Perhaps a clue is to be found beneath the car park of the house for it is believed that this covers the remains of Saint Andrews Church, one of the lost churches of Lewes. If the church stood here then so did its burial ground and it may be the spirit of the lady belongs to more ancient times.

35. LAW COURTS CELLS – ACID BATH MURDERER

Go up twitten to side of Rights of Man Pub and turn right down the lane

This twitten goes behind the law courts. The windows low down with bars on are the windows of the cells beneath the court rooms. Many famous murderers have sat in those cells when they were tried at Lewes Assizes. Perhaps the most evil and notorious was John Haig, the infamous acid bath murderer from Crawley. He murdered rich people then dissolved his victims' bodies in a vat of acid then forged their signatures so he could sell their possessions for his own gain. All that remained of them when he was caught was thick sludge embedded with human teeth and gold fillings and other human parts. Haig's confirmed victims numbered six but he claimed to have murdered three more which were never substantiated. Even more horrible, Haig claimed he had drunk the blood of his victims in his pleas of insanity presumably to escape the death sentence. He was hanged in Wandsworth prison on 10th August 1949.

36. THE LEWES ARMS – A FEW SPIRITS FOR THE ROAD

Continue to the Lewes Arms

The Lewes Arms could have two, maybe three spirits haunting its walls. Perhaps one of them is former Landlord John Spitsbury. He seems to have had a premonition of his demise. In November 1772 he ordered his coffin and named six of his fellow publicans as pall bearers. A few days later he was dead and buried at Saint Johns. The pub may also have its own guardian spirit which some of those who have lived or worked here call George. He appears to be somewhat temperamental;

Lewes Arms

some have described his presence as warm and protective, especially when alone at night in the building. But for those he takes a dislike to he can make life hell. At least two landlords have been driven out by his antics. He is said to throw objects about, turn beer taps on and off and, worst of all, turn the beer bad. He apparently behaves this way if a landlord he likes decides to leave the pub.

The spectre, which two staff encountered late one night after the pub had closed, may have been a different spirit. They were both sitting at the bar when they heard the sound of the front door open and close, although they had locked up. Both had the impression of a figure moving swiftly along the hallway, through the doorway that leads upstairs. They were both large men and unafraid but they were puzzled and concerned that there was an intruder. However, a search of the building showed no trace of anyone. They both returned to the bar and had no sooner sat down when they heard the sound of footsteps moving to and fro in the room above their heads. Again, they ran up the stairs and found the room and building deserted. This could be the same spirit that haunts the cellars here. On occasions the sound of a woman singing has been heard, she sings a strange unidentifiable tune. The sound does not actually appear to be coming from a point in the cellar but from a point in the earth behind its walls.

o here ends Legends of Lamplit Lewes. A collection of tales told by people, or those who wrote of them, which however fantastic they may seem, were all recounted or documented as true.

There are more stories of Lewes as yet untold, dark paths, as yet unwalked. Those are left for you gentle reader to discover, if you dare.

This is an ancient and beautiful town but beneath its streets and behind its walls still lurk many mysteries and histories dark, strange.

For now, may peace and sweet dreams come to you this night and wake safely in tomorrow's dawn.

REFERENCES

As mentioned in the forward, much of the research done to collect the stories for this walk was by Nick. Alas the original references and articles used to create the walk were not available. While checking the stories during editing this list of some wider possible reference materials of interest has been compiled. As mentioned in the Introduction, a few tales were also recorded from talking to people in local premises at the time.

Haunted places of Sussex: Judy Middleton, 2005

Haunted Sussex Today, Andrew Green, reprint from 2001

Sussex Ghost Stories, published by Bradwell Books, 1st edition

Hauntings and Ghosts of Sussex, Lucy May

East Sussex Ghosts: Robert A Stevens 1996 (revised 2013)

William and Gundrada story: local historical accounts, Wikipedia

Railway burial pit: local history accounts, https://sussexpast.co.uk/battle-of-lewes-main/landport-bottom-the-battlefield/the-battle-of-lewes-the-urban-battlefield, Handbook for Lewes, MA Lower (published 1845)

~ *References* ~

Southover Grange 'A Brief History' by A Milward Flack), Wikipedia

Spring Heeled Jack: Sussex Express Article ' Ghostly man with a spring in his step' 20th April 2013 and Wikipedia

Lewes Avalanche : Historic UK

https://www.historic-uk.com/HistoryUK/HistoryofBritain/Lewes-Snow-Drop-1836/ and local history accounts

Railway disaster : local history / Radio Sussex & Quirky Sussex History by Kevin Gordon, https://sussexhistory.net/2016/03/08/did-a-10yr-old-cause-a-train-crash/

Quirky Sussex History, Kevin Gordon https://sussexhistory.net/2019/11/26/railway-jack/

The Pinwell: https://folio.brighton.ac.uk/user/mg237/history-of-pinwell-street-the-lost-twitten

Pastfinder.com – Holy wells in Sussex

https://insearchofholywellsandhealingsprings.com

Miracle of the Fish - first recorded by LF Salzman in a volume of Sussex Archaelogical collections 1925

Lewes prison haunting: Mystical world wide web "Ghosts of Sussex"

Robert Brinkhurst murder story: http://www.brightonourstory.co.uk/ourstory-newsletters/lewes-murder/

Blacks Guide Books for Tourists- Sussex Adam and Charles Black

Tales and Readings for the People Volume 1, George Vickers, 1849